# Japanese
# Kimekomi

## Fast, Fun, and Fabulous
## Fabric Handballs

Barbara B. Suess    Kathleen M. Hewitt

*Breckling Press*

Library of Congress Cataloging-in-Publication Data

Suess, Barbara B.
  Japanese kimekomi : fast, fun, and fabulous fabric handballs / Barbara B.
Suess and Kathleen M. Hewitt.
    p. cm.
  ISBN 978-1-933308-21-0
  1.  Fancy work--Japan. 2.  Patchwork--Japan. 3.  Decorative balls--Japan.
I. Hewitt, Kathleen M. II. Title.

  TT751.S92 2008
  746.46'0410952--dc22


2008014812

Editorial and production direction by Anne Knudsen
Cover and interior design by  Maria Mann
Cover and interior photographs by Sharon Hoogstraten
Technical drawings by Barbara B. Suess and Kathleen M. Hewitt
This book was set in Hiroshige and Caecilia

Published by Breckling Press
283 N. Michigan St, Elmhurst, IL 60126
Printed and bound in China
International Standard Book Number: 978-1-933308-21-0

# Dedication

*To Betty and Elsie,*
*our mothers*

# Acknowledgements

*Our thanks go to Japanese craftsmen and craftswomen
for the skills they have taught us; our families, especially
Terry and Calvin; Mr. Miki, a generous friend and terrific
translator of Japanese; and our friends for their trust,
sharing, and support. A special thanks to the following
companies for their help: Dremel® and Robert Bosch
Tool Corporation, suppliers of the Dremel® Versa Tip™
Multipurpose Tool; and Plasteel Corporation, supplier of
Smoothfoam™ Expanded Polystyrene (EPS) balls.*

# Contents

# Preface

The history of kimekomi (pronounced *kee may ko mee*) dates back to the first half of the eighteenth century. It is believed that while working at the Kamo Shrine in Kyoto, a thrifty craftsman created the first dolls of their kind out of fabric scraps and willow tree wood found along the banks of the Kamo River. The dolls were carved so the edges of fabrics forming the clothing could be tucked into the grooves in the wood. These dolls were called *Kamo* dolls and the technique of making them became known as *kimekomi*, which translates as "a method of tucking something into a groove." Like many Japanese arts and crafts, the kimekomi technique was perfected and handed down through generations. Unique to the Kamo region, carved wooden Kamo dolls did not catch on and quickly disappeared; but in the nineteenth century a larger and more elaborate doll made using similar techniques gained popularity. It became known as the kimekomi doll. Still popular today, the dolls are manufactured from pressed wood and retain the round faces and body shapes that generations of Japanese people find so appealing.

How did the kimekomi technique transform from doll to ball? It could be that the round characteristics of kimekomi dolls inspired Japanese artisans to apply their dollmaking techniques to balls.

The designs in *Japanese Kimekomi* have their roots in Japanese culture, but also have a contemporary Western twist. While some of the designs may be found stitched on temari balls, for others we have drawn on the rich American tradition of patchwork quilt blocks to inspire new patterns. Requiring only a few materials and a little practice, Kimekomi is a fun, playful craft that allows you to be as creative as you wish! Enjoy!

# Kimekomi Basics

Kimekomi balls are pretty to look at, fun to hold, and—best of all—easy to make! The basic process consists of three simple stages: first, prep the smooth Styrofoam base by marking the design using the templates in the back of the book and cutting grooves; second, cover the ball with fabric and tuck it in the grooves; then, third, finish off with decorative trim. Pull out your fabric scraps and shop for some pretty trim, and you are halfway there. There are just a few more essential supplies, like smooth Styrofoam balls, a knife, a tucking tool, and glue. Get ready, get set, and go!

# Get Ready: Supply Kit

As with any craft, it always helps to clear a good working space and get your supplies in order before you start. This will make for smoother, faster ball-making, and lots more fun!

### Smooth Styrofoam Balls

Available from craft stores, an expanded polystyrene (EPS) ball holds up well when carving the grooves and tucking in the fabric. Ask for a smooth Styrofoam ball. We love Plasteel's EPS balls (see page 94) because they are dense yet easy to carve with the hot knife. Better still, they already have some of the markings you will need (such as the north pole, equator, and south pole) stamped onto the surface. Check the kimekomi pattern for the correct size ball before you head out shopping.

### Quilt Batting

To give kimekomi balls a soft, textured quality, a layer of batting is sandwiched between the smooth Styrofoam ball and the fabric. Use any scraps of medium-weight batting you have at hand—low-cost polyester works better than more costly cotton batting.

### Fabric Scraps or Fat Quarters

Any combination of colors and prints that pleases you will make lovely kimekomi balls. Cottons are easy to find and work great, but consider other textiles as well. Try sheer fabrics layered with non-transparent ones for an elegant touch. Make an "heirloom" ball from lovely old embroidered tea towels, pillow cases, or other inherited pieces you just can't throw away. Layer lace over a solid fabric for romance. You could also use the same décor fabrics that are already in your room and make a bowl of kimekomi balls to match. You can work with scraps, but if you purchase fabric, buy ¼ yard pieces or fat quarters and you will have plenty.

# Kimekomi Kit!

Smooth Styrofoam balls
Quilt batting
Fabric scraps or fat quarters
Trim
Glue
Tape measure

Markers
Carving tool
Sandpaper
Tracing materials
Tucking tool
Sewing awl or stylus

## Trim

It's good practice to finish adding fabric to your ball before auditioning trims to glue over the grooves. Feel free to use any yarn, cords, or other trims you find that compliment the colors already on your ball. Sometimes you will want to pick a strong color from your fabric and use a similar colored trim to make the design really "pop." Other times, it may be better to choose a softer shade trim which blends well with the fabric. Most of the balls in *Japanese Kimekomi* are trimmed with satin rattail cord, which is a rayon and cotton blend (see page 94).

# Keys to Kimekomi

These two diagrams on the right show two views of a ball: from the top and from the side. The north pole is, of course, the top of the ball; the south pole is the bottom; and the equator is a line around the fullest part of the ball.

An essential step in prepping a ball for a kimekomi design is to mark it into usable sections; the dashed lines here represent eight equal sections. (Think of them as the segments of an orange.) Several designs call for eight sections, while some need only four or six. Drawing these lines helps keep everything in balance, so that the top of your ball will exactly mirror the other side. The colored dots—in this case, yellow and purple—further identify precise points on the ball. For instance, here the yellow dots are exactly halfway between the pole and the equator; the purple dots are one fourth of the way from the equator. In most cases, you will not need to mark dots to determine shapes to carve. The dots are used mainly when you decide to resize the pattern and make a bigger or smaller ball. The little hash marks (l , ll, or lll) indicate measurements: lengths are equal if the number of hash marks is equal; lengths are not equal if the number of hash marks differs. If you are using the size indicated in the pattern, you will not

## Glue

You may use any brand of glue stick to adhere a layer of batting to the smooth Styrofoam. For the trim, use fabric glue or craft glue. Since this step requires a steady hand, look for a squeeze bottle with a fine-tip opening.

## Other Essentials

Beyond basic craft tools like scissors, an iron, pencils, and pins, you will need:

* Tape measure: ¼" or 0.5 cm wide, marked with inches and centimeters. If you can, purchase one that is made of cloth or slightly textured fiberglass; it will "hug'" the ball and not slip.

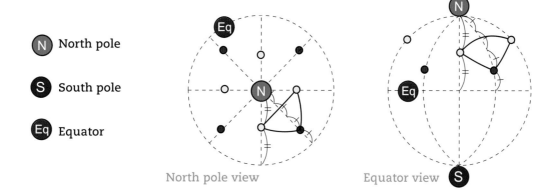

North pole | North pole view
South pole | Equator view
Equator

need to use the hash marks. The solid black line shows the most important lines on the ball—the lines you will carve to create a design. As you can see, they form a solid line from dot to dot.

If you are making balls the same size called for in each pattern, you will use the templates at the back of the book. The solid black lines on the templates are for marking directly onto the smooth Styrofoam ball and for cutting batting. The dashed lines are for cutting fabric. Note that the batting pieces are smaller than the fabric pieces because the batting is not tucked into the grooves. The fabric templates include an allowance for tucking.

- Markers: Use a fine-tip permanent marker to draw the design onto the ball. Use a marker or a #2 pencil to transfer template shapes onto the fabric. Keep a bottle of white-out correction fluid in your tool kit to cover up mistakes or disguise any lines that show through light fabrics.

- Carving tool: A hot knife is the best tool for carving the grooves in a smooth Styrofoam ball. This small plug-in appliance carves lines effortlessly and smoothly (see resources on page 94 for brand information). The next-best option is an X-acto knife or equivalent with a #11 fine point precision blade.

- Sandpaper: Use fine grit sandpaper for smoothing rough carved ridges.

- Tracing materials: Use tracing paper, wax paper, plastic bags, or lightweight interfacing to trace the templates or to make new templates.

- Tucking tool: Anything goes! Try a small, blunt-edged knife, a butter knife, an artist's palette knife, a small screw driver, a nail file, or a letter opener.

- Sewing awl or embossing tool (stylus): A fine-tip awl helps to smooth wrinkled edges, straighten the fabric around tight angles, or remove excess glue.

# Get Set: Ten Easy Steps

To a beginner, kimekomi designs may look complicated, but once you understand how they are put together, you will immediately see how simple they are! The secrets to even, consistent patterns is in the ball-prep. Once you know the basics, you can tackle any of the patterns in *Japanese Kimekomi* with confidence! These ten simple steps will take you there.

## Mark Section Lines

1  Pin a tape measure to the ball around the equator, with the centimeter marks next to the equator line. Divide the length of the equator by the number of sections required in the pattern. For example, let's say you have a 3" ball with 24 cm circumference (the equator measurement). To create four sections, divide 24 by 4 to make 6. With a marking pen, draw dots around the equator every 6 cm. Remove the tape measure.

# Making a Slip Knot

Form a loop at one end of the thread with end A in front of end B. Holding the threads at the crossover in your left hand, use the fingers of your right hand to go through the loop, from front to back, and grab at the center of end A as shown at the blue circle. Now hold both ends of the thread in your left hand and pull the new loop, held with your right hand, through the center of the first loop. Place the new loop around the shaft of a pin. Tighten by pulling on end A. When you are finished using the knot, remove it from the pin and simply pull on both ends of the thread to release it.

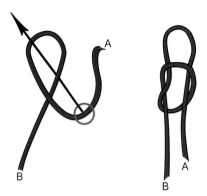

2 Starting at the north pole, lay the tape measure in a straight line to a dot on the equator. Mark with a dashed line along the edge. Continue in a straight line around the ball, past the south pole and back up to the north pole, marking with a dashed line as you go. Repeat with the remaining dots on the equator, moving around the ball and making more dashed lines from pole to pole. You may have to pin the tape measure to the ball if you find it slipping.

An alternate way to draw the section lines is to use a heavy thread such as perle cotton or fine yarn. Place a pin at the north pole. At one end of the thread make a slip knot and secure it to the pin (see above). Lay the thread down on the ball in a straight line from north pole to a dot at the equator and then on to south pole. Draw a dashed section line using the thread as a guide. Rotate the thread around the pin to draw remaining section lines on the ball.

# Fussy Cutting Fabric to Add a Motif

Give a ball a particular theme by including a particular motif cut from fabric. You will need to cut carefully to make sure the chosen motif fits nicely on the ball. *Picture Window* (see page 19) begins with a ball marked in 8 segments, then the design is marked and carved. The second photo shows how the pattern pieces are positioned for cutting. In the third photo, *Picture Window* is complete.

## Mark the Carving Lines

3 Following the pattern you have selected and using the templates at the back of the book, mark the carving lines onto the ball. (Use the solid black lines; the dashed lines are for cutting fabric only.) Keep in mind that you will be applying flat templates to a round ball. Small templates will usually fit nicely on the ball but larger ones may bunch a little. To mark accurately, pin the template to the ball or press your fingers flat against it as you mark. Unless otherwise noted in the instructions, mark around templates at the south pole as if they were mirror images of the north pole, using the same section lines to orient the template.

Note that each design offers the option of resizing to suit a smaller or larger ball. Directions for marking the ball are included with the pattern.

# Making Your Own Templates for Resized Balls

After you've drawn the carving lines on the ball following the optional resizing instructions provided with the pattern, you'll need to make batting and fabric templates for the bigger or smaller ball. This is quick and easy to do.

First, place the ball in a clear plastic bag (like a food storage bag). Make sure the plastic fits smoothly and neatly over one of the shapes needed for a template. Take care not to stretch the plastic or it will alter the contour of the template. If the shape is large, pin the plastic to the ball to hold it in place. Trace the shape on the plastic bag with a marking pen and take the ball out of the bag. Now, your plastic bag has a batting template drawn on one side.

To draw the fabric template, flip the bag over. You can see the batting template on the other side of the bag. Draw a dashed line about $3/8$" to $1/2$" outside the batting template around each side. Voilà! You have your fabric template on one side of the plastic bag and your batting template on the other side.

Repeat with all the shapes needed to create the kimekomi design. At this point, you may like to transfer the templates from the plastic to a see-through medium such as tracing or wax paper before cutting out batting and fabric. Cut out the templates, labeling the right side of each one as you go.

## Carve the Ball

4 Using a hot knife or X-acto knife, carve grooves along the solid carving lines marked in the previous step. Be sure to follow all directions that come with the tool, especially those regarding safety. If using a hot knife, work in a well-ventilated area. Cut into the ball to a depth of $1/2$" to $5/8$" on a 3" or larger ball. On smaller balls, use less of the blade for a shallower cut.

Holding the bottom half of the ball with your hand, slowly and carefully rotate it away from you as you carve in a controlled motion. Try to keep the knife blade above the ball, maintaining a consistent position. To maneuver around tight curves, you may need to use a sawing or up-and-down motion. After carving, make sure the grooves are clean and even by drawing an awl or tucking tool through the groove. Lightly sand away any rough spots from the ball's surface.

# Cutting Fabric Shapes

*Asymmetrical shapes* must be cut with the fabric right side up for them to fit properly on the ball.

*Symmetrical shapes* may be cut two or more pieces at a time by layering or folding fabric to reach the desired number of pieces.

*Mirror image shapes* are cut by placing just one pattern piece on a folded piece of fabric. When you cut, the two resulting pieces will mirror-image each other.

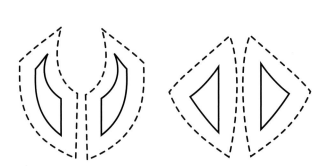

## *Prepare the Batting and Fabric*

5  Trace the batting and fabric templates for your selected design. You can use tracing paper, wax paper, plastic bags, or light-weight interfacing. If you prefer, photocopy the pattern pieces.

6 Pin the templates to the fabric and, using the dashed lines, cut the number of pieces called for in the directions. Take care to fit any special design elements or motifs in the fabric at the center of the template. Using the solid lines of the template, cut a piece of batting to go with each fabric piece.

## Decorate the Ball

7 Working with one shape at a time, dab an office-type glue stick on a shape on the ball and center the corresponding batting piece in place. This will fit neatly onto the ball, with no need to tuck the batting down into the grooves. When you've completed a few kimekomi balls, you may decide to skip the step of gluing the batting to the ball. Just hold it in place and continue to the next step.

8 Make sure each fabric piece is wrinkle-free. Center a fabric piece over the corresponding batting piece. With a tucking tool, tuck only the fabric into the carved grooves of the ball. Always hold fabric and batting pieces firmly in place with one hand while you tuck with the other. If you've tucked the fabric down into the grooves all around one shape and have more than about ⅛" of fabric peeking out of the grooves, use small, sharp scissors to trim away the excess fabric. Continue to tuck the rest of the fabric into the grooves.

This partly completed ball, *Wrapped Bands*, still shows the carving lines and the batting

# Neat and Tidy Trim!

A little preplanning helps give a neat appearance to the trim.
When you are finished adding the trim, you should not see any
starts and stops. This may require hiding some ends under trim
that has already been applied or leaving an end unglued until
another section of trim is applied underneath it. In most cases,
start by trimming the shorter lines, then longer lines, and finally
the lines that wrap all the way around the ball.

**9** Use a sewing awl or an embossing tool to neaten up your lines. Slide
it along the grooves to straighten the fabric and to get fabric edges all
tucked nicely out of sight. Getting neat corners is somewhat like making
a bed; redistribute any excess fabric by drawing it away from each corner.
Smooth down the sides using the awl or embossing tool. Continue adding
batting and fabric to each shape until the ball is covered.

## Add Trim

**10** Begin by tucking the tail end of the trim about ¼" (0.5 cm) down into
the groove at an intersection. An awl or embossing tool is very useful
for this step. Working with a few inches at a time, apply a small line of
glue over the grooves of the path you wish to trim. Lay the trim over the
groove, carefully removing any excess glue as you work. A fingernail, awl,
or embossing tool works well to remove excess glue. Keep your hands and
tools glue-free as much as you can. Cut the trim ¼" (0.5 cm) beyond the
length needed and tuck in the remaining end.

# Option: Add a Hanger

If you are making Christmas tree ornaments or wish to hang your finished kimekomi ball, it's easy to add a hanging loop. Cut a piece of cord 5" long. Open up a ½"-deep space in the ball for the hanger by using an awl or other pointed tool. Apply a generous amount of glue into the hole and use the awl to tuck in both ends of the cord. (Since Plasteel's Smoothfoam brand balls have one pole with a large hole, consider using that pole for the top of the ball.)

# Go!

In *Japanese Kimekomi* there are 15 ball designs to choose from, as well as a unique pattern for Easter-egg making. The patterns are arranged in order of difficulty. Start off with one of the earlier patterns and you will be on your way! As needed, refer back to this section for extra help. Enjoy!

# Reflections

*Easy to draw and quick to carve,* Reflections
*is the simplest kimekomi ball to make. It requires
no special template or marking, since the section
lines themselves form the design. Select fabrics that
coordinate in theme and color.*

*Before you begin, read through the pattern
instructions carefully. Also, read or review Kimekomi
Basics at the beginning of the book. Pay special
attention to the ten steps for completing each design
on pages 6 to 12. You will find the template for
this design on page 83.*

## Supplies

**3" ball**
**Fabric #1:** Cut 8, Template A
**Fabric #2:** Cut 8, Template A
**Trim:** 2½ yards

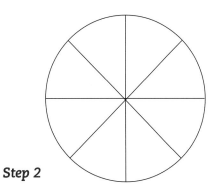

**Step 2**

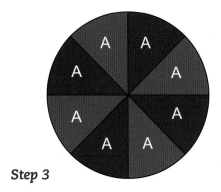

**Step 3**

**1** Mark the ball into eight equal sections with a solid line (see page 6, Steps 1 and 2). Mark the equator with a solid line. There are now 16 distinct triangles on the ball.

**2** Carve along the marked section lines, then carve around the equator (see page 9, Step 4).

**3** Decorate the ball by applying batting and fabric (see page 10, Steps 5 to 9).

**4** Add trim (see page 12, Step 10).

# Playtime!

## Variations

- There are 16 triangles on this kimekomi. You may use two fabrics, alternating sections as shown. Or why not use many different fabrics, one in each triangle, as a jazzy alternative?

- Experiment with pattern by using curved lines instead of straight lines and see what happens! This variation is shown in the photograph on page 16.

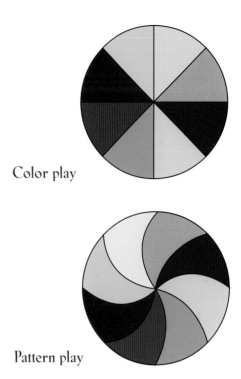

Color play

Pattern play

## Extra Option: Resize the Ball

It's easy to vary the size of this design. Just mark your ball into eight sections, then add the equator line. Trace the segments to make templates for cutting fabric. (See page 9.)

# Picture Window

Picture Window *is ideal for showcasing special motif fabrics in kimekomi balls. Who wouldn't love these teddy bears? All this requires is a simple technique known as fussy cutting, where you carefully center the template over your chosen motif before you cut (see also page 8). Here, we fussy cut just four fabric squares, using complimentary fabrics for the rest of the ball.*

*Before you begin, read through the pattern instructions carefully. Also, read or review Kimekomi Basics at the beginning of the book. Pay special attention to the ten steps for completing each design on pages 6 to 12. You will find the templates for this design on page 83.*

## Supplies

**3" ball**

**Fabric #1:** Cut 8, Template A

**Fabric #2:** Cut 4, Template B (theme fabric)

**Trim:** 2 yards

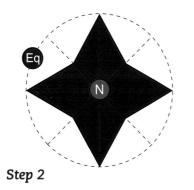

**Step 2**

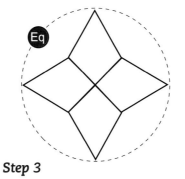

**Step 3**

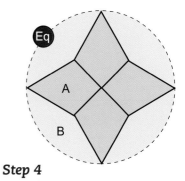

**Step 4**

**1** Mark the ball into eight equal sections (see page 6, Steps 1 and 2). Mark the equator.

**2** Lay Template A on the ball with one point at the north pole and the opposite point at the equator; mark around the template (see page 8, Step 3). Reposition and mark around Template A three more times around the north pole and four times around the south pole. For clarity, the template is shown here in red.

**3** Carve the ball as shown (see page 9, Step 4). Do not carve the equator. You will end up with four square picture windows around the equator.

**4** Decorate the ball by applying batting and fabric (see page 10, Steps 5 to 9).

**5** Add trim (see page 12, Step 10).

# Playtime!

## Variations

- Personalize *Picture Window* by putting hand or machine-embroidered words on the "window" pieces instead of teddy bears or other motifs. You might add a name, a date, and/or a special occasion so that your gift becomes a cherished family heirloom.

- To create a more intricate ball, try dividing the square picture window into four triangles and dividing the kite shapes around the poles in half. Play with different fabric combinations for a fun, colorful ball.

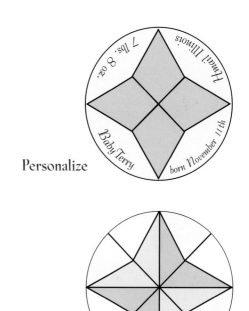

Personalize

Pattern play

## Extra Option: Resize the Ball

To draw this design on a larger or smaller ball, draw dots one half of the distance from the equator to the north pole on every other section line. Draw dots one half of the distance from the equator to the south pole on the same section lines. Draw the pattern shapes by connecting the dots with equator intersections as shown in red.

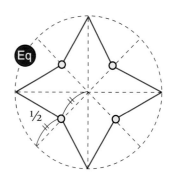

Resize

# Mosaic

Mosaics are like puzzles. They are beautiful to look at when finished, but the process of completing one is the ultimate joy. Each piece is no less important to the beauty of a mosaic than another, and so it is with each and every thing that touches our lives.

Before you begin, read through the pattern instructions carefully. Also, read or review Kimekomi Basics at the beginning of the book. Pay special attention to the ten steps for completing each design on pages 6 to 12. You will find the templates for this design on page 84.

## Supplies

**2½" ball**
**Fabric #1:** Cut 6, Template A
**Fabric #2:** Cut 8, Template B
**Trim:** 1¼ yards

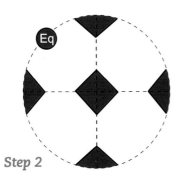

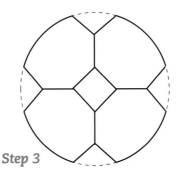

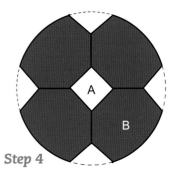

Step 2        Step 3        Step 4

1 Mark the ball into four equal sections (see page 6, Steps 1 and 2). Mark the equator.

2 Place a pin through the center dot of Template A and attach to the ball where any two lines intersect; mark around the template as shown in red (see page 8, Step 3). Repeat for the remaining five intersections.

3 Carve the ball as shown (see page 9, Step 4). Do not carve the equator. You will end up with six small squares and eight large hexagons.

4 Decorate the ball by applying batting and fabric (see page 10, Steps 5 to 9).

5 Add trim (see page 12, Step 10).

# Playtime!

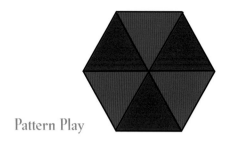

## Variations

● Consider dividing the hexagons into smaller shapes like these triangles for a more intricate mosaic.

● Similar to *Picture Window* on page 19, this design also has a large open area, perfect for fussy cutting a theme or motif fabric. Make a treasured heirloom by adding inherited embroidered pieces to the large shapes on the ball.

**Pattern Play**

## Extra Option: Resize the Ball

To draw this design on a larger or smaller ball, measure the distance from one of the poles to the equator line. Divide by 7, then multiply by 2. Measure that exact result outward from each intersection, then draw dots. Draw six squares by connecting the dots, as shown in red.

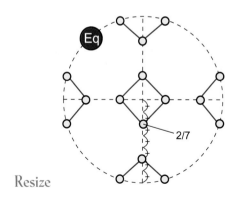

**Resize**

# Hydrangea

The motif depicted in this kimekomi ball is found in art design throughout the world, sometimes serving as the background for other designs. Here we chose a lovely hydrangea print fabric. You will find the curves are as easy to carve as straight lines when using a hot knife.

Before you begin, read through the pattern instructions carefully. Also, read or review Kimekomi Basics at the beginning of the book. Pay special attention to the ten steps for completing each design on pages 6 to 12. You will find the templates for this design on page 84.

## Supplies

**3" ball**
**Fabric #1:** Cut 12, Template A
**Fabric #2:** Cut 8, Template B
**Trim:** 2 yards

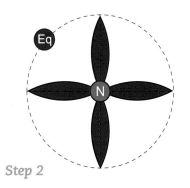

Step 2

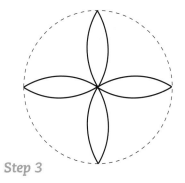

Step 3

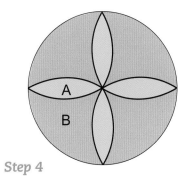

Step 4

1 Mark the ball into four equal sections (see page 6, Steps 1 and 2). Mark the equator.

2 Lay Template A on the ball. Line up the points with the intersections. Mark around the template (see page 8, Step 3). Reposition and mark a total of twelve petal shapes: four each around the north pole, south pole, and equator.

3 Carve the ball as shown (see page 9, Step 4).
Do not carve the equator. You will end up with twelve petal shapes and eight open spaces between them.

4 Decorate the ball by applying batting and fabric (see page 10, Steps 5 to 9).

5 Add trim (see page 12, Step 10).

# Playtime!

## Variations

- Use several solid pastels for a Spring kimekomi ball. What a lovely Easter gift it would make!

- Divide the petals in half lengthwise and fill with two different shades of green to make the leaves more lifelike.

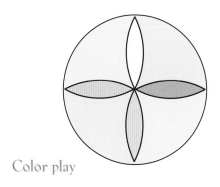

Color play

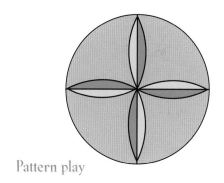

Pattern play

## Extra Option: Resize the Ball

To draw the design onto a larger or smaller ball, measure the distance between the equator and the north pole. Draw a petal shape of this length for Template A. Trace the space between the petals to make Template B.

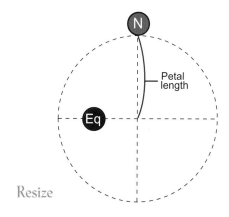

Resize

# Wrapped Bands

Inspired by a traditional Japanese temari ball design, Wrapped Bands *is striking in its simplicity. Template A is provided as a guide for you to draw the bands, but you could also lay a thin tape measure along each section line and use its edge as a guide for drawing.*

*Before you begin, read through the pattern instructions carefully. Also, read or review Kimekomi Basics at the beginning of the book. Pay special attention to the ten steps for completing each design on pages 6 to 12. You will find the templates for this design on pages 84 to 85.*

## Supplies

3" ball
**Fabric #1:** Cut 6, Template B
**Fabric #2:** Cut 8, Template C
**Fabric #3:** Cut 12, Template D
**Trim:** 2¼ yards

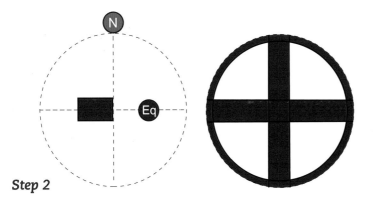

**Step 2**

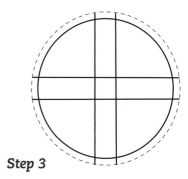

**Step 3**

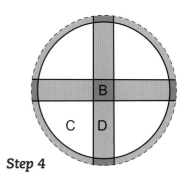

**1** Mark the ball into four equal sections (see page 6, Steps 1 and 2). Mark the equator.

**2** Lay Template A on the ball along the equator line; mark along the long edges (see page 8, Step 3). Reposition Template A around the equator and mark to create a band wrapping all the way around the ball. Make bands around the other two section lines on the ball in the same way.

**Step 4**

**3** Carve the ball as shown (see page 9, Step 4). Do not carve the equator. You will end up with six small squares, twelve rectangles, and eight triangle shapes.

**4** Decorate the ball by applying batting and fabric (see page 10, Steps 5 to 9).

**5** Add trim (see page 12, Step 10).

# Playtime!

## Variations

- Imitate the style of Frank Lloyd Wright by carving each of the bands into smaller pieces.

- Use the same fabrics on three different balls, but switch their positions. For example, exchange the rectangle shape fabric with the triangle shape fabric.

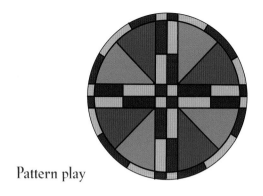

Pattern play

## Extra Option: Resize the Ball

To draw the design onto a larger or smaller ball, draw a line above and below the equator. The exact width of the band doesn't matter so long as it is pleasing to your eye. Draw the same width bands around the section lines.

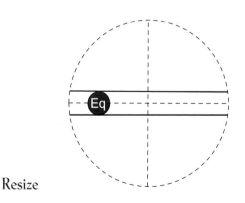

Resize

# Queens' Cup

A darling wildflower found growing from Alaska to California, Queens' Cup is a violet-shaded member of the lily family. The curves of the templates illustrate the flower's delicate nature.

Before you begin, read through the pattern instructions carefully. Also, read or review Kimekomi Basics at the beginning of the book. Pay special attention to the ten steps for completing each design on pages 6 to 12. You will find the templates for this design on page 85.

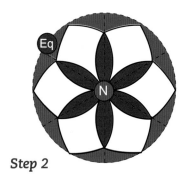

**Step 2**

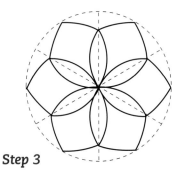

**Step 3**

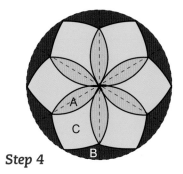

**Step 4**

**1** Mark the ball into six equal sections (see page 6, Steps 1 and 2). Mark the equator.

**2** Lay Template A on the ball with one end at the north pole; mark around it (see page 8, Step 3). Reposition the template, still with one end at the north pole, and mark around it five more times, as shown in red. Repeat six more times at the south pole. Lay Template B along the equator so that top and bottom points touch the points of A; mark around it. Reposition the template and mark around it five more times, as shown in blue.

**3** Carve the ball as shown (see page 9, Step 4). Do not carve the equator.

**4** Decorate the ball by applying batting and fabric (see page 10, Steps 5 to 9).

**5** Add trim (see page 12, Step 10).

# Playtime!

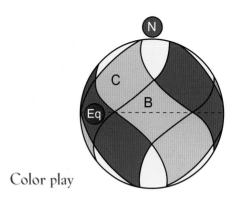

Color play

## Variations

- Leave the flower petals all filled with the same color. Alter the color of the fabrics for Templates B and C for a completely different look.

- Divide each shape in half lengthwise and fill them each with two different shades of the same color fabric.

Pattern play

## Extra Option: Resize the Ball

To draw the design onto a larger or smaller ball, draw a dot one fourth of the distance from the equator to the pole. Draw a petal shape this length for Template A. Draw a gentle curve from the points of the petals to the equator line to form Templates B and C.

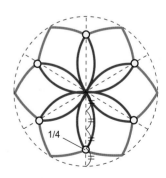

Resize

# Primroses

A harbinger of spring, primroses bring delight with their bright and cheerful colors. Decorate your home with these balls during the spring season or surprise someone with an Easter basket of "primroses."

Before you begin, read through the pattern instructions carefully. Also, read or review Kimekomi Basics at the beginning of the book. Pay special attention to the ten steps for completing each design on pages 6 to 12. You will find the templates for this design on page 86.

## Supplies

**3" ball**
**Fabric #1:** Cut 12, Template A
**Fabric #2, 3, 4:** Cut 8, Template B
**Trim:** 2¾ yards

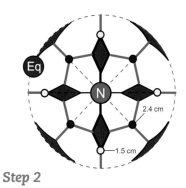

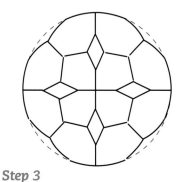

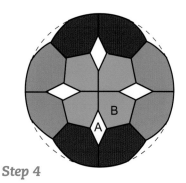

**Step 2**                    **Step 3**                    **Step 4**

**1** Mark the ball into eight equal sections (see page 6, Steps 1 and 2). Mark the equator.

**2** On the north pole side, draw a dot 1.5 cm above the equator on every other section line, as shown in yellow. Lay Template A on a section line with a narrow point on a dot, extending its body toward the north pole; mark around the template (see page 8, Step 3). Repeat three more times to form four diamonds around the north pole as shown in red. Repeat at the south pole side.

 Lay Template A on the remaining section lines, with its narrow points on the equator line; mark around the template. Repeat three more times to form four diamonds around the equator.  On section lines intersecting diamonds at the equator, draw dots 2.4 cm from the equator, as shown in purple. Draw connecting lines from the dots to diamond points, as shown in blue. Repeat at the south pole side. The ball will have six flowers, each with four petals.

**3** Carve the ball as shown (see page 9, Step 4). Note that only parts of the equator and section lines are carved.

**4** Decorate the ball by applying batting and fabric (see page 10, Steps 5 to 9).

**5**  Add trim (see page 12, Step 10).

**40**     PRIMROSES

# Playtime!

## Variations

- Experiment in adapting the design by simply changing the fabric layout on the ball.

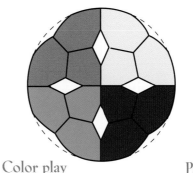

Color play

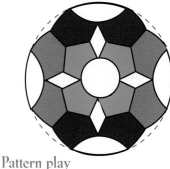

Pattern play

- Connect the diamonds with a circle inside each petal to create an interesting geometric design. Do you see a kaleidoscope?

## Extra Option: Resize the Ball

To draw the design onto a larger or smaller ball, begin by drawing dots one fourth of the distance from the equator to each pole on every other section line, as shown in yellow. Draw a diamond template using the diagram as a guide. Cut out the template. Lay a narrow point of the template on each dot, extending its body to the closest pole; mark around the diamond template, as shown in red. Repeat on the south pole side. Lay the template on the remaining section lines with its narrow points on the equator line; mark around the template. On section lines containing diamonds at the equator, draw dots two-fifths of the distance from the equator to each pole, as shown in purple. Add connecting lines as shown in blue from purple dots to points of diamonds to form six flowers with four petals.

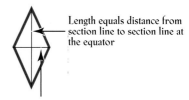

Length equals distance from section line to section line at the equator

Width equals one tenth of the distance from the equator to pole

Draw diamond template

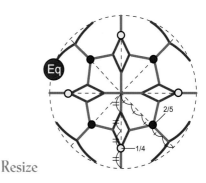

Resize

# Starry Path

*Dreamers often look to celestial forms in the sky for inspiration. Place this quilt-inspired ball in a conspicuous location to remind you of your dreams and challenge you to reach for the "starry paths."*

*Before you begin, read through the pattern instructions carefully. Also, read or review Kimekomi Basics at the beginning of the book. Pay special attention to the ten steps for completing each design on pages 6 to 12. You will find the templates for this design on page 86.*

## Supplies

**3" ball**
**Fabric #1, 2:** Cut 4, Template A
**Fabric #3:** Cut 8, Template B
**Fabric #4:** Cut 8, Template C
**Trim:** 2 1/3 yards

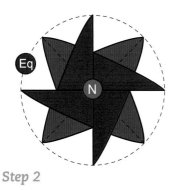

Step 2

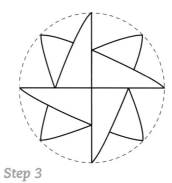

Step 3

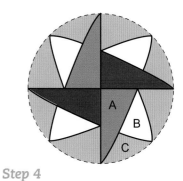

Step 4

1 Mark the ball into eight equal sections (see page 6, Steps 1 and 2). Mark the equator.

2 Lay Template A at the north pole so that the narrow points touch the equator; mark around the template. Repeat three more times around the north pole, as shown in red (see page 8, Step 3). Lay Template B on a section line below a Template A shape so that the points touch the equator, as shown in blue; mark around the template. Repeat three more times. Draw the same design on the south pole side.

3 Carve the ball as shown (see page 9, Step 4). Do not carve the equator line.

4 Decorate the ball by applying batting and fabric (see page 10, Steps 5 to 9).

5 Add trim (see page 12, Step 10).

# Playtime!

## Variation

- Take a close look at the 8-point star diagram below. Play with combining shapes to create a number of different designs.

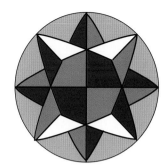

Pattern play

## Extra Option: Resize the Ball

To draw the design onto a larger or smaller ball, begin by drawing dots halfway from pole to equator on each section line, as shown in yellow. Draw an 8-point star, as shown in red. The first line begins at #1, passes through dots at #4 and #7, and ends at #2. The line will have a slight curve on the ball. Continue, in the same fashion, connecting other points from #2 to #3, #3 to #4, and so on until you finish at #1. Repeat on the south pole side.

The shapes shown in this design are created by combining section lines and 8-point star segments. Do not carve the equator. Retrace the outlines of the shapes with a solid line or a different colored marking pen so that you can clearly see which lines to carve.

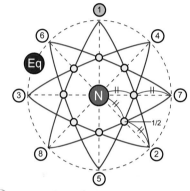

Resize: Draw an 8-point star

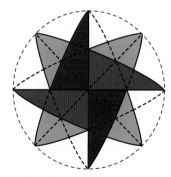

Resize: Draw the design

# Carolina Favorite

This old fashioned quilt block was introduced by the Old Chelsea Station Needlecraft Service. The gracefulness of this design reminds us of our personal fondness of spring in the Carolinas.

Before you begin, read through the pattern instructions carefully. Also, read or review Kimekomi Basics at the beginning of the book. Pay special attention to the ten steps for completing each design on pages 6 to 12. You will find the templates for this design on page 87.

## Supplies

**3" ball**
**Fabric #1,2:** Cut 4, Template B
Cut 4, Template D
Cut 4, Template E
Cut 4, Template F
Cut 4, Template G
**Fabric #3:** Cut 8, Template H
Cut 8, Template I
**Trim:** 3⅓ yards

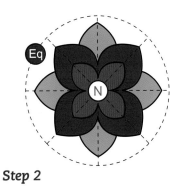

**Step 2**

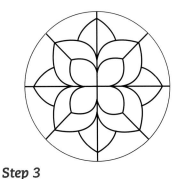

**Step 3**

**Step 4**

**1** Mark the ball into eight equal sections (see page 6, Steps 1 and 2). Mark the equator.

**2** Lay Template A at the north pole; mark around the template (see page 8, Step 3). Repeat three more times, creating four petals around the pole, as shown in red. Lay Pattern B over the red petals at the north pole; mark around the template. Repeat three more times, creating four inner petals, as shown in blue. Lay Template C between two red petals, with the points about 0.5 cm from the equator; mark around the template. Repeat three more times, creating four outer petals, as shown in green. Draw the same design on the south pole side of the ball.

**3** Carve the ball as shown (see page 9, Step 4). Carve around the equator.

**4** Decorate the ball by applying batting and fabric (see page 10, Steps 5 to 9).

**5** Add trim (see page 12, Step 10).

# Playtime!

## Variation

- You'll get a different look from the same design by mixing up the color scheme. A black or dark background and/or trim will add drama to both bright and pastel colored fabrics.

Color play

## Extra Option: Resize the Ball

To draw the design onto a larger or smaller ball, begin with the inner petals. Draw dots one sixth of the distance from the pole to the equator on every other section line, as shown in yellow. Draw dots one half the distance from pole to the equator on the remaining section lines, as shown in purple. Connect the dots by drawing four small petals, as shown in blue.

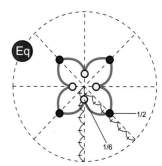

Resize: Inner petals

Next, draw the middle and outer petals. Draw dots five-sixths of the distance from the pole to the equator, as shown in yellow. Draw dots one third of the distance from the pole to the equator, as shown in purple. Connect dots by drawing four middle petals, as shown in red. Draw dots 0.5 cm from the equator on every other section line, as shown in red. Draw four petals, as shown in green.

Repeat the previous steps for the south pole.

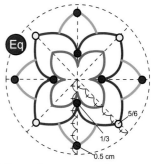

Resize: Middle and outer petals

# Hearts & Diamonds

Celebrate an anniversary, wedding, or Valentine's Day with this festive heart ball or just give it to someone very special any time of year.

Before you begin, read through the pattern instructions carefully. Also, read or review Kimekomi Basics at the beginning of the book. Pay special attention to the ten steps for completing each design on pages 6 to 12. You will find the templates for this design on page 88.

## Supplies

3" ball

**Fabric #1:** Cut 2, Template E

Cut 8, Template F

Cut 8, Template G

**Fabric #2:** Cut 8, Template C

**Fabric #3:** Cut 8, Template D

**Fabric #4:** Cut 4, Template B

**Trim for heart:** 2 yards

**Trim for diamond frame:** 1⅛ yards

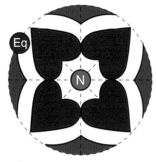

**Step 2**

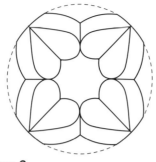

**Step 3**

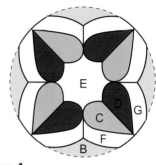

**Step 4**

**1** Mark the ball into eight equal sections (see page 6, Steps 1 and 2). Mark the equator.

**2** On the north pole side of the ball, lay heart Template A on every other section line, as shown in red. The bottom points of the heart will touch the equator line; mark around the template (see page 8, Step 3). Repeat on the south pole side. Lay Template B on the remaining section lines so that the points touch the equator and the section lines, as shown in blue; mark around the template.

**3** Carve the ball as shown (see page 9, Step 4). Notice that parts of the equator and section lines are carved.

**4** Decorate the ball by applying batting and fabric (see page 10, Steps 5 to 9).

**5** Add trim (see page 12, Step 10). Using two different colors of trim allows each design element, hearts and diamonds, to stand out.

# Playtime!

## Variations

- Make a butterfly ball using the mirrored hearts and frames just by changing the fabric scheme and adding additional trim for antennae.

- Exclude marking the carving lines from diamond Template B and use the curve of the hearts to form larger diamond shapes. Fill the larger diamond shapes with a beautiful print fabric.

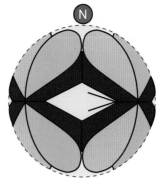

Color play

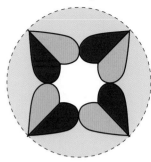

Pattern play

## Extra Option: Resize the Ball

To draw the design onto a larger or smaller ball, first draw the diamonds. Around every other intersection along the equator, draw four dots: Draw the first two dots two-thirds of the distance from the intersection on the equator line, as shown in yellow; draw two dots one fourth of the distance from the intersection on the section line, as shown in purple. Draw four diamonds around the equator by connecting the four dots, as shown in blue.

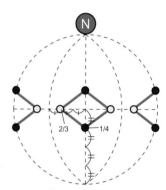

Resize: Draw diamonds

Cut a square piece of paper with the length and width three fourths of the length of a section line from the pole to the equator (square size = distance from pole to equator x 0.75). Fold the paper in half and cut half a heart shape. Use as much of the paper square as possible to create the heart shape. Unfold the paper and lay the heart template on the ball with the fold over one section line, as shown in red; mark around the template. Repeat for the remaining hearts at both poles.

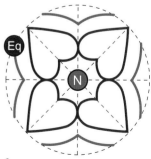

Resize: Draw hearts

# Shasta Daisy

Summer-blooming Shasta daisies look at you with golden eyes surrounded by many slender white petals. The daisy gets its name from "day's eye" since it tends to close its petals after sunset. The Shasta daisy is named for the famous Mt. Shasta in California.

Before you begin, read through the pattern instructions carefully. Also, read or review Kimekomi Basics at the beginning of the book. Pay special attention to the ten steps for completing each design on pages 6 to 12. You will find the templates for this design on pages 88 to 89.

## Supplies

**4" ball**

**Fabric #1:** Cut 8, Template A
Cut 8, Template C
Cut 8, Template D
Cut 8, Template E

**Fabric #2:** Cut 8, Template A
Cut 8, Template C
Cut 8, Template D
Cut 8, Template E

**Trim:** 4½ yards

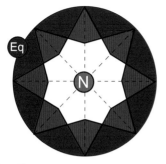

**Step 2**

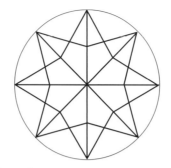

**Step 3**

**Step 4**

**1** Mark the ball into eight equal sections (see page 6, Steps 1 and 2).

**2** Lay Template A on the ball along the equator between two section lines; mark around the template (see page 8, Step 3). Reposition Template A around the equator, marking its shape between remaining pairs of section lines, as shown in red. Lay Template B between each of the red shapes; mark around the top edges, shown in blue. Draw the same design on the south pole side of the ball.

**3** Carve the ball as shown (see page 9, Step 4).

**4** Decorate the ball by applying batting and fabric (see page 10, Steps 5 to 9).

**5** Add trim (see page 12, Step 10).

# Playtime!

## Variations

- Tuck different soft-hued batik fabrics into each shape on the ball to create a dreamy, Impressionist sampler.

- Draw the pattern on the ball and then select different lines to carve.

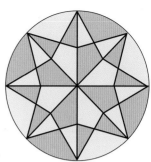

Color play

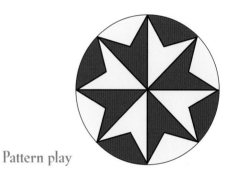

Pattern play

## Extra Option: Resize the Ball

To draw the design onto a larger or smaller ball, first draw a dot one half of the distance between the equator and north pole on each section line. Next, draw an X in each section, connecting the dots and the equator intersections. Draw the same design on the south pole side.

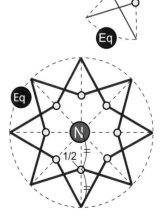

Resize

# Mariner's Compass

Mariner's Compass *is one of the oldest quilt designs known in America, very likely inspired by the navigational instrument used by sailors to find their way around the high seas. A true mariner's compass has 16 or 32 sections but begin with this easier, 8-section version.*

*Before you begin, read through the pattern instructions carefully. Also, read or review Kimekomi Basics at the beginning of the book. Pay special attention to the ten steps for completing each design on pages 6 to 12. You will find the templates for this design on pages 89 to 90.*

## Supplies

**3" ball**
**Fabric #1:** *Cut 1, Template D*
*Cut 8, Template E*
*Cut 8, Template G*
**Fabric #2**: *Cut 8, Template F*
*Cut 8, Template H*
**Fabric #3**: *Cut 8, Template I*
*Cut 8, Template J*
**Trim:** 3 yards

**Step 2**

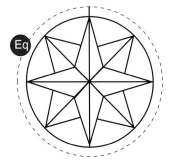

**Step 3**

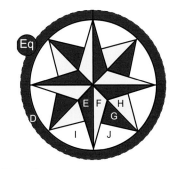

**Step 4**

1 Mark the ball into eight equal sections (see page 6, Steps 1 and 2). Mark the equator.

2 Lay Template A next to the equator to draw the band that wraps around the equator, as shown in red; mark around the template (see page 8, Step 3). Lay Template B with one point at the north pole; mark around it. Reposition and mark around Template B a total of four times, as shown in blue. Next, lay Template C between the blue shapes, with its bottom point on the band around the equator, as shown in green; mark around the template. Draw the same design on the south pole side of the ball.

3 Carve the ball as shown (see page 9, Step 4). Do not carve the equator line.

4 Decorate the ball by applying batting and fabric (see page 10, Steps 5 to 9).

5 Add trim (see page 12, Step 10).

*16–section variation*

# Playtime!

## Variations

- Use the colors of the flag for a patriotic design.

- Omit parts of the section lines to create a simpler design. Divide the band around the equator into rectangles.

Color play

Pattern play

## Extra Option: Resize the Ball

To draw the design onto a larger or smaller ball, first draw a line 1 cm above and below the equator line to form a band around the equator, as shown in red. Measure the distance from the edge of the band to the north pole. Draw dots one third of this distance from the north pole on every other section line. Draw lines connecting the dots with the band as shown in blue. Next, using the same one third measurement, draw dots as shown in red along the blue lines. Draw lines connecting the dots to the band around the equator, as shown in green. Repeat on the south pole side.

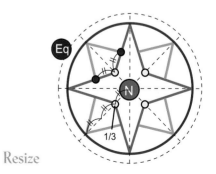

Resize

# Sunflower

From Van Gogh's paintings to Chihuly's sculptured glass ikebana installations, sunflowers have long been a dramatic subject matter for artists' works in all media. Here's your chance to be the artist!

Before you begin, read through the pattern instructions carefully. Also, read or review Kimekomi Basics at the beginning of the book. Pay special attention to the ten steps for completing each design on pages 6 to 12. You will find the templates for this design on pages 90 to 91.

## Supplies

**4" ball**
**Fabric #1:** Cut 2, Template A
**Fabric #2:** Cut 10, Template B
**Fabric #3:** Cut 20, Template D
**Fabric #4:** Cut 20, Template E
**Fabric #5:** Cut 20, Template F
**Trim:** 4 1/8 yards

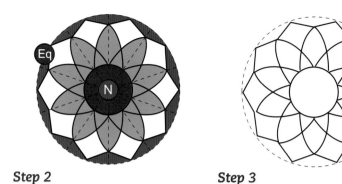

**Step 2**

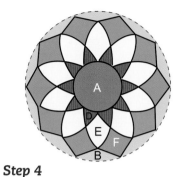

**Step 4**

**1** Mark the ball into ten equal sections (see page 6, Steps 1 and 2). Mark the equator.

**2** Place a pin through the center of Template A and attach it to the north pole, as shown in red; mark around the template (see page 8, Step 3). Lay Template B on a section line and along the equator, as shown in blue; mark around it. Repeat nine more times to create a series of diamond shapes around the equator. Lay Template C over a section line between the red circle and blue diamonds; mark around it. Repeat nine more times on each section line. Markings from Template C will overlap each other around the ball. Draw the same design on the south pole side.

**3** Carve the ball as shown (see page 9, Step 4). Do not carve the equator line.

**4** Decorate the ball by applying batting and fabric (see page 10, Steps 5 to 9).

**5** Add trim (see page 12, Step 10).

# Playtime!

## Variations

- Use alternating jewel tone prints on diamond shapes to create a harlequin effect. Celebrate Mardi Gras with golds, greens or purples.

- Sunflower petals are made by carving two swirling lines in opposite directions. If you don't carve the right to left swirl, you will have a completely new design with a spiraling effect, as shown in the diagram.

## Extra Option: Resize the Ball

To draw the design onto a larger or smaller ball, first draw dots two thirds of the distance from the equator to the north pole on every section line, as shown in yellow. Draw a circle around the north pole by connecting yellow dots, as shown in red. Draw dots one sixth of the distance from the equator to the north pole on every section line, as shown in purple. Measure one half of the distance between section lines along the equator and draw dots, as shown in red. Connect the purple and red dots, forming a zigzag pattern around the ball, as shown in blue. Create flower petals by drawing an X in between section lines from the yellow dots to the purple dots, as shown in green. Create a gentle curve to each line. Repeat at the south pole. Ten diamond shapes will form on the equator line.

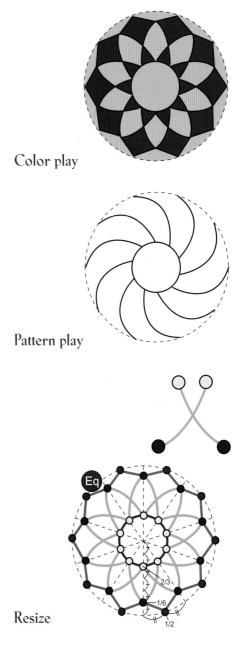

Color play

Pattern play

Resize

# Seashells

The half circles formed by this design are quite familiar to Japan and are meant to represent the waters of the seas and oceans. Often used as a background for other motifs, this design is prevalent in the Japanese arts. Quilters from the western hemisphere refer to this design in many ways such as seashell, clamshell, fish scale, and sugar scoop.

Before you begin, read through the pattern instructions carefully. Also, read or review Kimekomi Basics at the beginning of the book. Pay special attention to the ten steps for completing each design on pages 6 to 12. You will find the templates for this design on pages 91 to 92.

## Supplies

4" ball
**Fabric #1 & 2:** Cut 8, Template A
Cut 8, Template C
**Fabric #3**: Cut 16, Template B
**Fabric #4**: Cut 2, Template D
**Trim:** 3½ yards

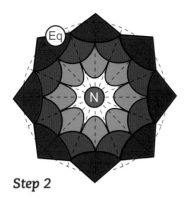

Step 2

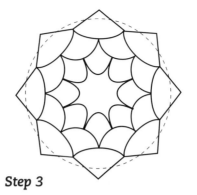

Step 3

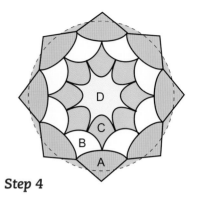

Step 4

**1** Mark the ball into 16 equal sections (see page 6, Steps 1 and 2). Mark the equator.

**2** Lay Template A on ball, matching up section and equator lines; mark around the template (see page 8, Step 3). Reposition and mark around the template seven more times around the ball, as shown in red. Lay Template B above and between the red shapes, matching section lines on the template and the ball; mark around the template. Repeat seven more times, as shown in blue. Lay Template C above and between the blue shapes, matching section lines on the template and the ball; mark around the template. Repeat seven more times, as shown in green. Draw the same design on the south pole side of the ball.

**3** Carve the ball as shown (see page 9, Step 4). Do not carve the equator line.

**4** Decorate the ball by applying batting and fabric (see page 10, Steps 5 to 9).

**5** Add trim (see page 12, Step 10).

# Playtime!

## Variation

- Change fabric colors and turn this ball into a cabbage rose or ocean waves design.

## Extra Options: Resize the Ball

To draw the design onto a larger or smaller ball, draw dots one eighth of the distance from the equator to the north pole on all section lines, alternating above and below the equator as shown in yellow. Draw a zigzag around the equator, connecting yellow dots to form the bottom part of the shells. Draw dots as shown in purple one fourth of the distance from the equator to the north pole on all section lines previously marked with dots below the equator. Draw a curved line with the peak at the purple dot, as shown in red. Eight large shells wrap around the equator.

To draw the middle row of medium shells, draw dots as shown in yellow one half of the distance between the equator and the north pole on section lines resting between two red shells in row 1. Draw a curved line with the peak at the yellow dot, as shown in blue.

To draw the final row of small shells, draw dots as shown in red three fourths of the distance from the equator to the north pole on section lines, resting between two blue shells in row 2. Draw a curved line with the peak at the red dot, as shown in green. Draw the same design on the south pole side of the ball.

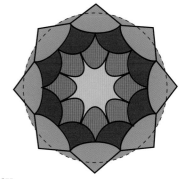

Color play

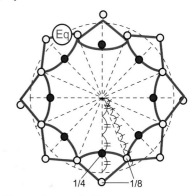

Resize: Draw large shells

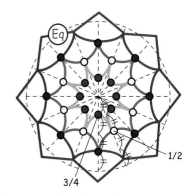

Resize: Draw medium/small shells

# Sun Goddess

The Sun Goddess, Amaterasu, shines brightly from heaven in Japanese mythology. The Imperial Family is said to be descended from Amaterasu, whose light was pure soul-warming comfort. This kimekomi ball design is based on a quilt block called Sunburst. When it is converted onto a ball, a beautiful combination of diamond and triangle shapes emerges around the equator.

Before you begin, read through the pattern instructions carefully. Also, read or review Kimekomi Basics at the beginning of the book. Pay special attention to the ten steps for completing each design on pages 6 to 12. You will find the templates for this design on pages 91 and 92.

## Supplies

**4" ball**

**Fabric #1:** Cut 8, Template B
Cut 8, Template G
Cut 16, Template H
Cut 16, Template I

**Fabric #2:** Cut 8, Template C
Cut 8, Template D
Cut 16, Template E
Cut 2, Template F

**Trim:** 5½ yards

**Step 2**

**Step 3**

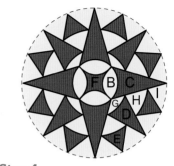

**Step 4**

**1** Mark the ball into 16 equal sections (see page 6, Steps 1 and 2). Mark the equator.

**2** Place a pin through the center of Template A and attach it to the north pole; mark around the template (see page 8, Step 3). Lay Template B inside the circle with one side lined up with Template A marking, as shown in red; mark around the template. Reposition and mark three more times around the north pole. Lay Template C with points on two sections lines, as shown in blue; mark around the template. Reposition and mark three more times. Lay Template D with points on two section lines as shown in green; mark around the template. Reposition and mark three more times. Lay Template E with points on two section lines as shown in yellow; mark around the template. Reposition and mark seven more times. Draw the same design on the south pole side of the ball.

**3** Carve the ball as shown (see page 9, Step 4). Do not carve the equator line.

**4** Decorate the ball by applying batting and fabric (see page 10, Steps 5 to 9).

**5** Add trim (see page 12, Step 10).

# Playtime!

## Variations

• As shown, the design uses just two fabrics. Change the look of the ball by adding alternate shades of each color, either lighter or darker, for a multi-fabric ball.

• Make the design easier by omitting some of the carving lines.

## Resize the Ball

To draw the design onto a larger or smaller ball, draw red dots two-thirds of the distance from the equator to the north pole on every section line. Draw a circle around the north pole by connecting the red dots. Draw lines connecting the edge of the circle with the equator, as shown in green. Draw four curved lines inside the red circle, as shown in blue. Divide each leg of the green star into thirds. Draw purple dots two-thirds of the distance from the equator along each leg of the green star. Connect the purple dots and equator intersections to form the star points, as shown in purple. Draw orange dots one third of the distance from the equator along each leg of the green star. Draw orange dots one half of the distance from the equator along each leg of the purple star. Connect the orange dots and equator intersections to form the star points, as shown in orange. Draw the same design on the south pole side of the ball.

Color play

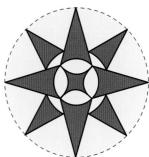
Pattern play

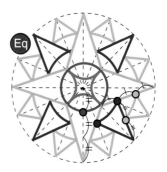
Resize

# Easter Eggs

Select an assortment of spring fabrics to cover eggs for a special Easter basket. While you are starting with a different shape, the technique is exactly the same.

Before you begin, read through the pattern instructions carefully. Also, read or review Kimekomi Basics at the beginning of the book. Pay special attention to the ten steps for completing each design on pages 6 to 12. You will find the templates for this design on page 93.

## Supplies

**2, 3, or 4" egg**
**Fabric #1:**
Cut 4, Template A (top)
Cut 4, Template B (bottom)
**Trim:** 1 yard

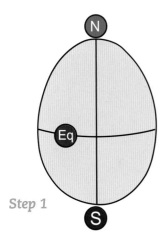
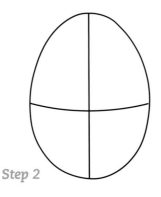
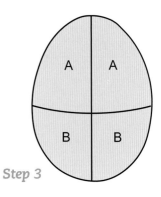

Step 1  Step 2  Step 3

**1** Mark the egg into 4 equal sections. Mark the equator. Draw section lines on the egg the same way you would if working on a ball—measure around the equator and divide it into four sections, then draw vertical lines around the poles (see page 6, Steps 1 to 3). The section lines are the carving lines in this simple design.

**2** Carve the egg as shown (see page 9, Step 4). Carve the equator line.

**3** Decorate the egg by applying batting and fabric (see page 10, Steps 5 to 9).

**4** Add trim (see page 12, Step 10).

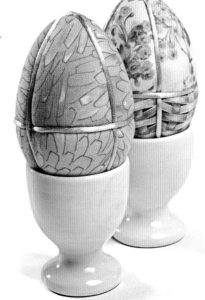

# Playtime!

## Variations

- Combine complimentary colors.

- Fill a top and bottom section with the same fabric. You can omit the equator, if you choose.

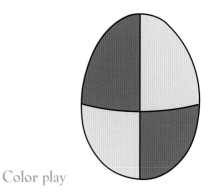

Color play

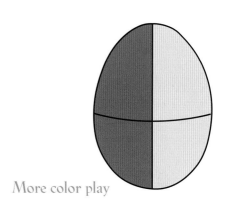

More color play

## Resize the Egg

This design easily transfers to any size egg. Just use the four section lines and the equator to make your patterns for a larger or smaller egg.

# Ball Games!

We hope the kimekomi ball designs in this book have inspired you to unleash your creativity and make many unique decorations for your home and charming gifts for friends and family. Here you will find more ideas to work with, as well as help in locating supplies and finding out more about kimekomi and other Japanese craft traditions.

# Simple Inspirations

There are many other Smoothfoam™ shapes that you can carve and tuck with fabric. Bells, hearts, cones, and miniature balls can all be made into fun decorations using the kimekomi method of applying fabric. You can also try free-form carving. Draw your initials, a flower, a Christmas tree or a gingerbread man shape on a ball. Carve and tuck in fabric for an extra-special holiday decoration or ornamental gift.

Many traditional Japanese kimekomi balls (and dolls) are covered with brocade or crepe fabric. Apply these elegant fabrics to your balls for an exotic look. Be inspired by other fabrics to create art-deco, country, graphic, or Impressionist kimekomi balls. Collect special textiles as you travel and vacation to start a collection of keepsake travel kimekomi balls.

The trim you add to a kimekomi ball is an important finishing touch that can dictate the style and mood of your craft. Add glitzy metallic cord for holiday decorations or rickrack on a county-style ball for just the right touch. Use multiple trims on a crazy quilt kimekomi ball. And why not make one of the designs in the book in all white fabrics with pearls as trim? You'll have a keepsake for a bride and groom or for wedding guests.

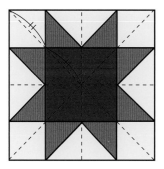

Original quilt block design

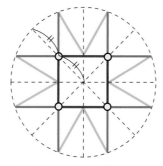

Marking the ball

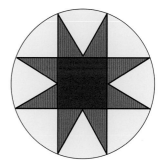

*Evening Star* kimekomi ball

# Convert Quilt Block Designs to Balls

A book filled with quilt blocks is a great place to begin when creating new kimekomi ball designs. If you've made a quilt, transform its blocks into circles, and use the fabric scraps to make a bowlful of kimekomi balls to match.

*Evening Star* is a favorite block among quilters. Notice in the first diagram how the corners of the center red square are halfway between the center and corners of the quilt block. To change the square block design to a circle, draw dots one half of the distance between pole and equator on every other section line. Draw a square by connecting the dots, as shown in red. Extend the sides of the square straight out to the equator line as shown in blue. Finish the star points as shown in green. The *Evening Star* quilt block design has been converted to a kimekomi design.

An attractive alternative for many quilt blocks is to first draw a band around the equator, then draw the block as shown.

# Templates

NOTE: Use the solid lines to mark the design on the ball and/or cut batting; use the dashed lines to cut fabric.

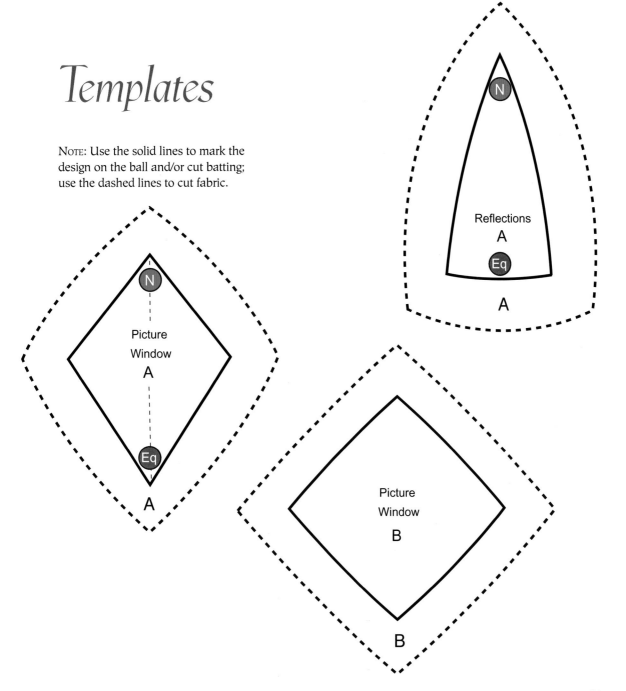

Reflections
A

A

Picture
Window
A

A

Picture
Window
B

B

NOTE: Use the solid lines to mark the design on the ball and/or cut batting; use the dashed lines to cut fabric.

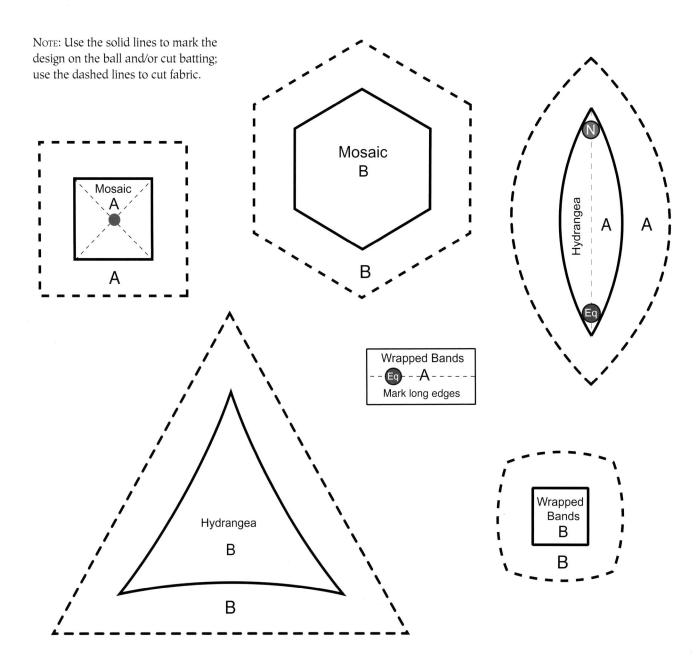

Mosaic
A

A

Mosaic
B

B

Hydrangea    A    A

N

Eq

Wrapped Bands
Eq — A
Mark long edges

Hydrangea
B

B

Wrapped
Bands
B

B

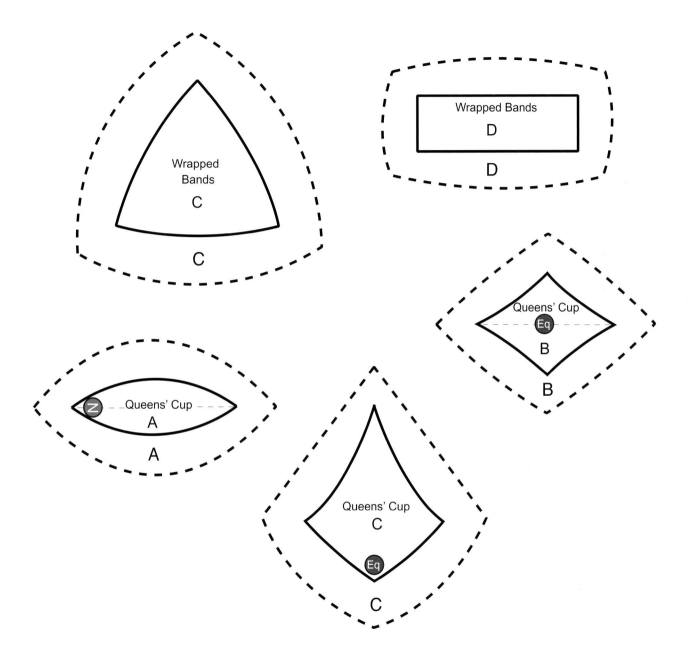

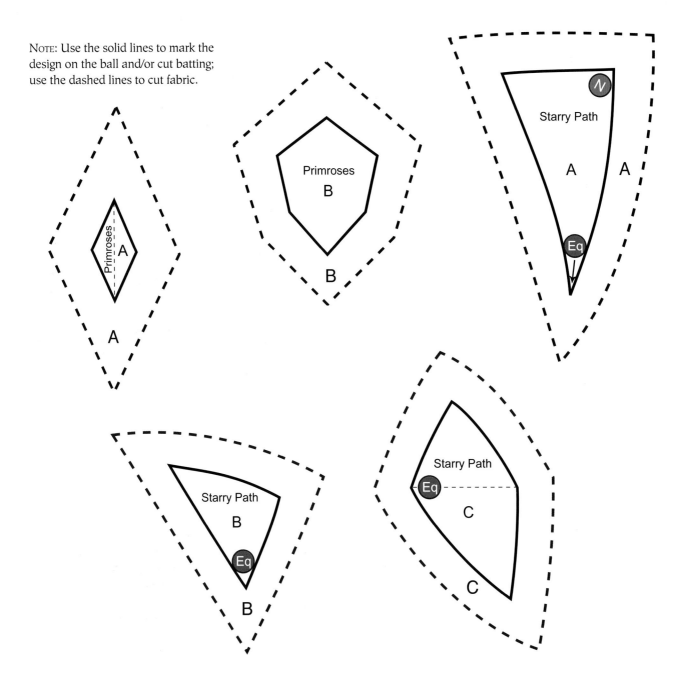

NOTE: Use the solid lines to mark the design on the ball and/or cut batting; use the dashed lines to cut fabric.

Primroses
A

Primroses
B

B

Starry Path
A

A

Starry Path
B

B

Starry Path
C

C

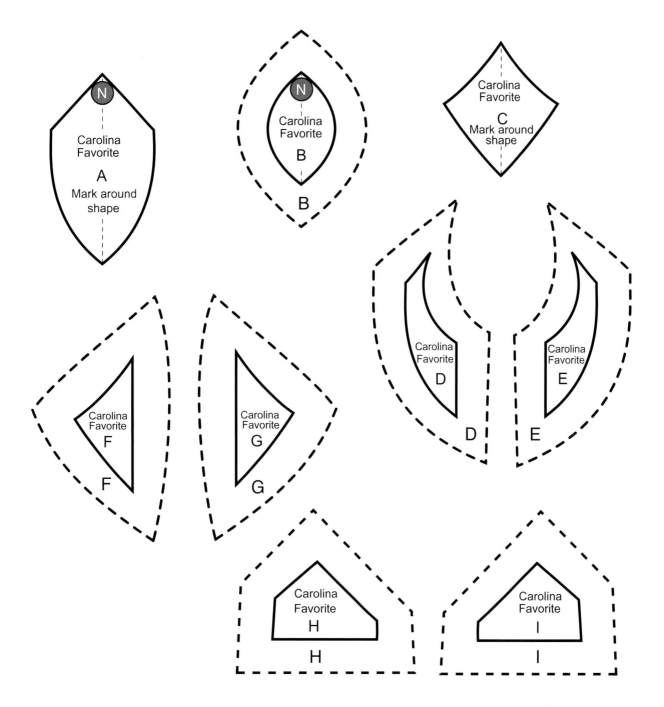

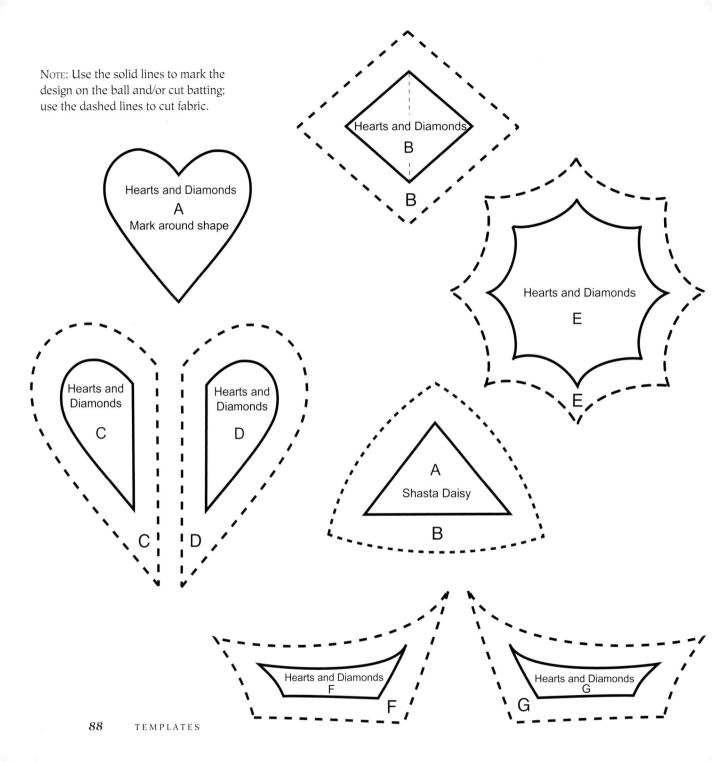

NOTE: Use the solid lines to mark the design on the ball and/or cut batting; use the dashed lines to cut fabric.

Hearts and Diamonds
B
B

Hearts and Diamonds
A
Mark around shape

Hearts and Diamonds
E
E

Hearts and Diamonds
C
C

Hearts and Diamonds
D
D

A
Shasta Daisy
B

Hearts and Diamonds
F
F

Hearts and Diamonds
G
G

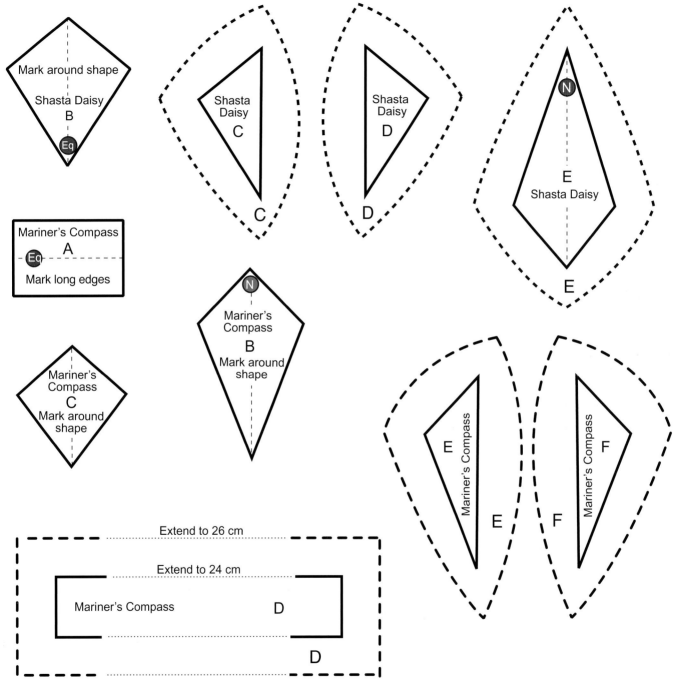

Mark around shape

Shasta Daisy

B

Eq

Shasta Daisy

C

C

Shasta Daisy

D

D

N

E

Shasta Daisy

E

Mariner's Compass

A

Eq

Mark long edges

N

Mariner's Compass

B

Mark around shape

Mariner's Compass

C

Mark around shape

Mariner's Compass

E

E

Mariner's Compass

F

F

Extend to 26 cm

Extend to 24 cm

Mariner's Compass

D

D

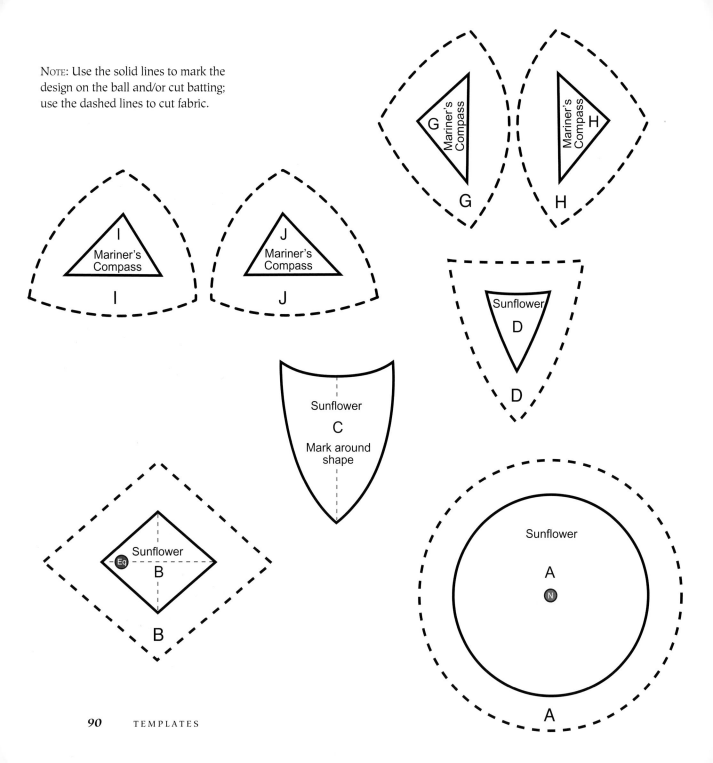

NOTE: Use the solid lines to mark the design on the ball and/or cut batting; use the dashed lines to cut fabric.

G
Mariner's Compass
G

H
Mariner's Compass
H

I
Mariner's Compass
I

J
Mariner's Compass
J

Sunflower
D
D

Sunflower
C
Mark around shape

Sunflower
B
Eq
B

Sunflower
A
N
A

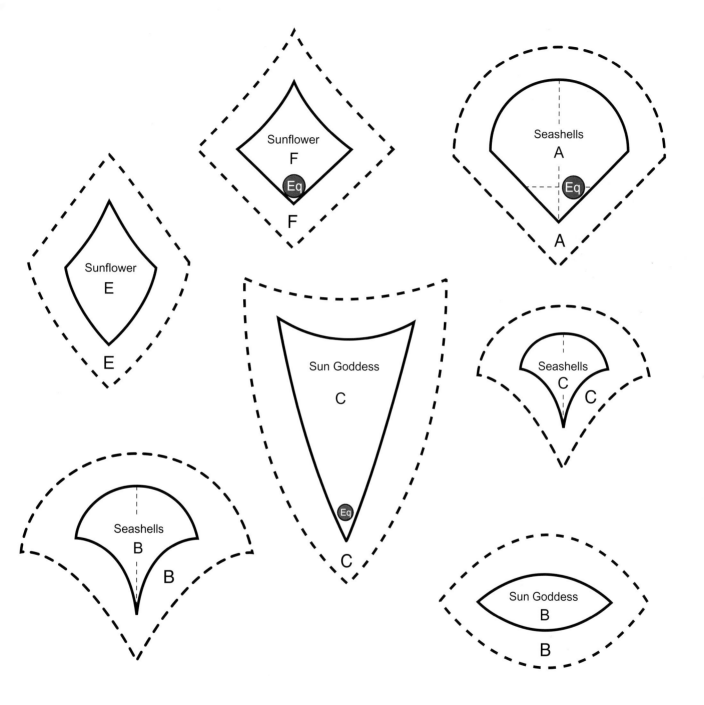

Sunflower
F

F

Seashells
A
Eq

A

Sunflower
E

E

Sun Goddess
C

Eq

C

Seashells
C
C

Seashells
B
B

Sun Goddess
B

B

NOTE: Use the solid lines to mark the design on the ball and/or cut batting; use the dashed lines to cut fabric.

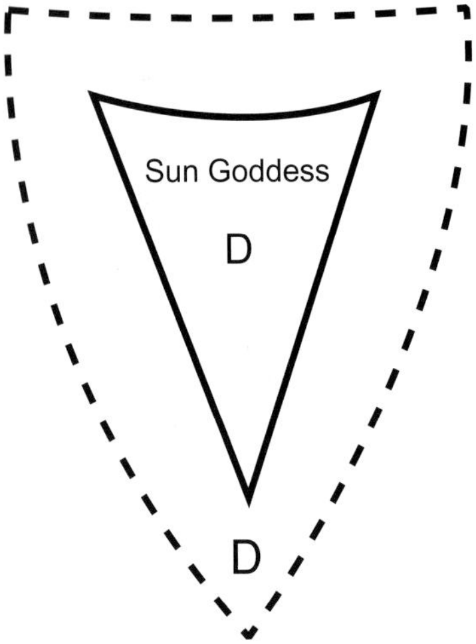

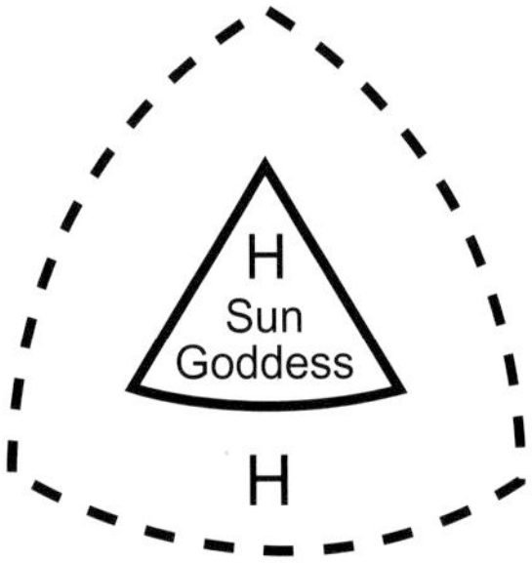

Sun Goddess

D

D

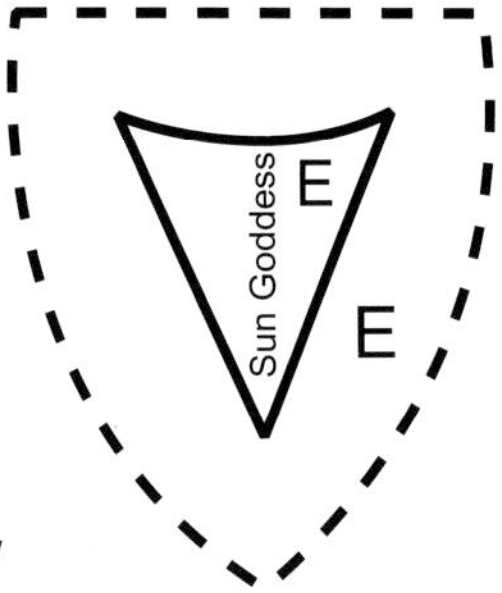

Sun Goddess

E

E

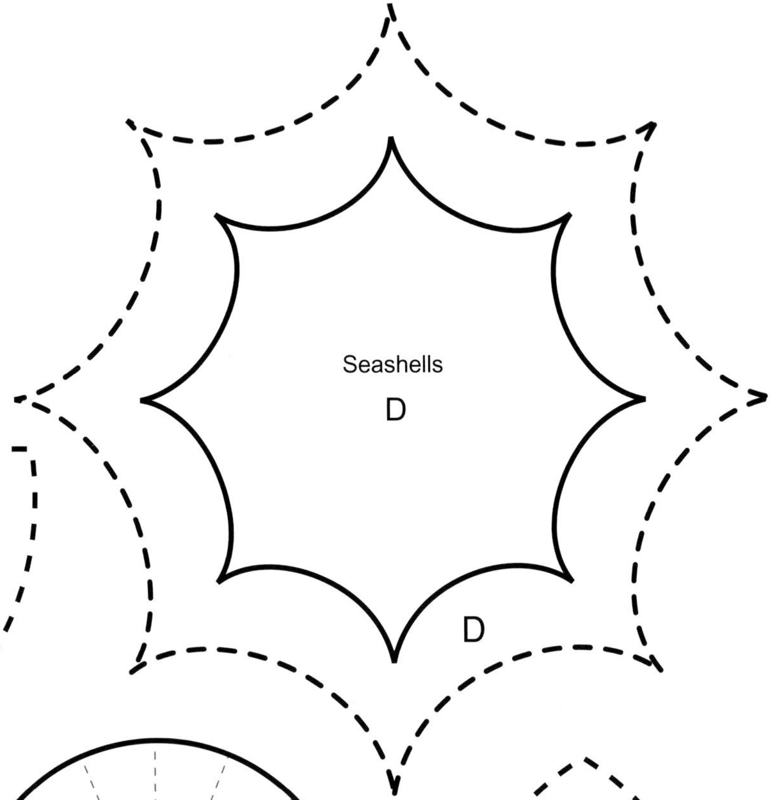

Seashells

D

D

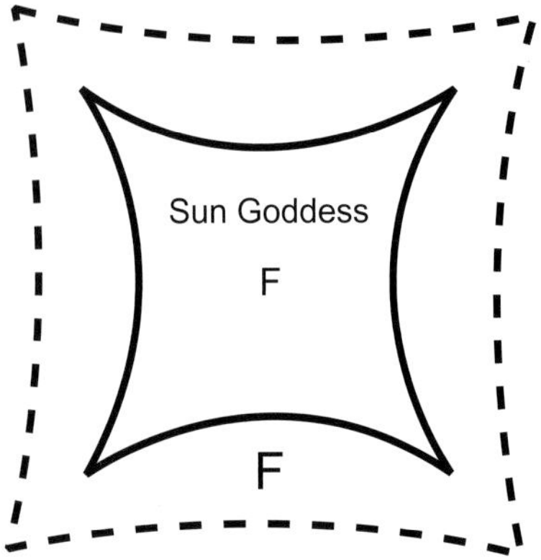

Sun Goddess

F

F

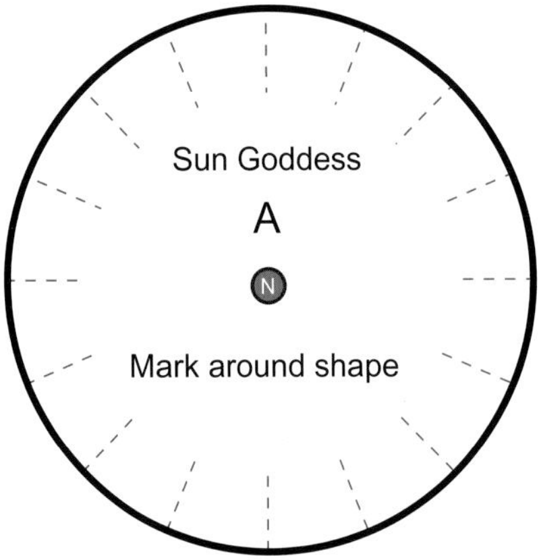

Sun Goddess

A

Mark around shape

H
Sun Goddess

H

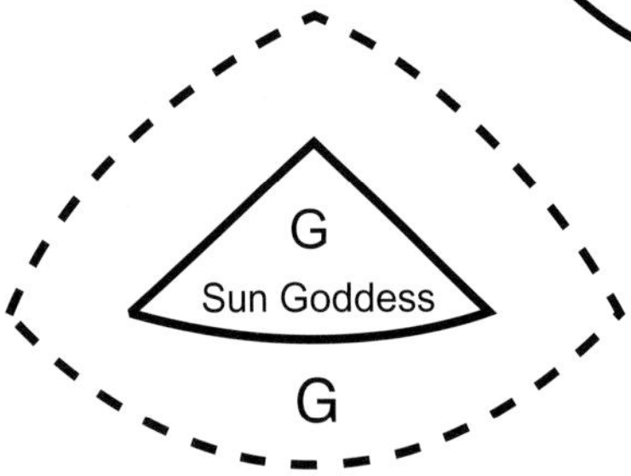

G
Sun Goddess

G

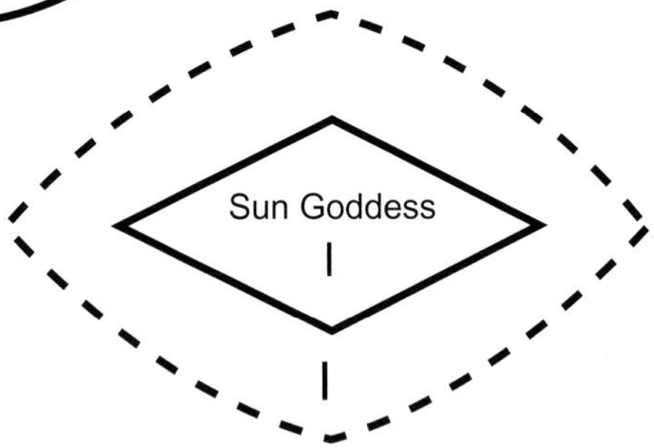

Sun Goddess

I

I

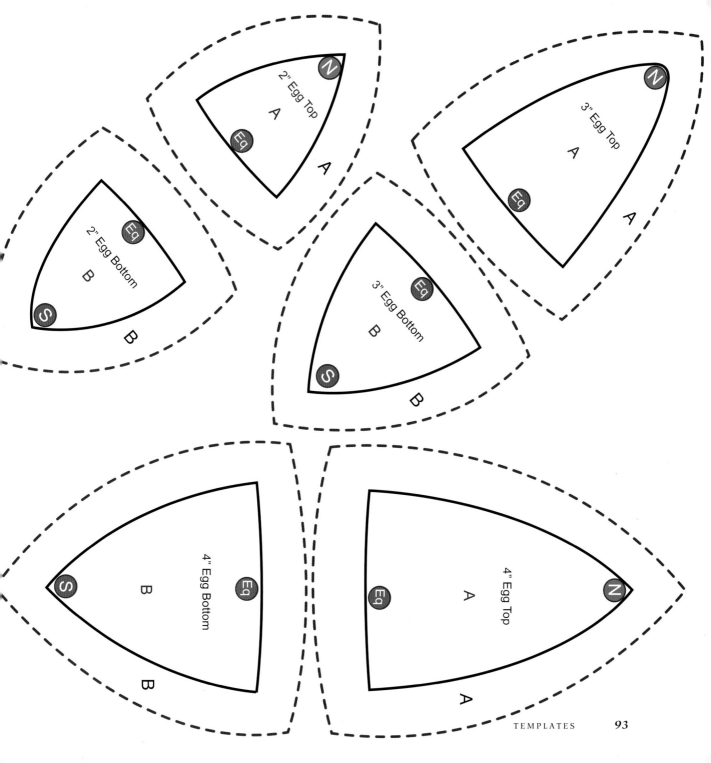

2" Egg Top

A

A

2" Egg Bottom

B

B

3" Egg Top

A

A

3" Egg Bottom

B

B

4" Egg Bottom

B

B

4" Egg Top

A

A

# Resources

## Essential Supplies

EPS balls, eggs, and other shapes:
Smoothfoam™ (www.plasteelcorp.com)

Hot knife tool:
Dremel 1550 Versa-Tip™ Multipurpose
Tool Kit (www.dremel.com) or Creative
Versa-Tool™ (www.walnuthollow.com)

Glue for applying trim:
Adhesive Tech™, A Fine Line (available
online and at some discount or craft stores)

Satin (Rattail) Cord:
La Stella Celeste (www.satincord.com)

## References

Baird, Merrily. *Symbols of Japan: Thematic
Motifs in Art and Design*. New York: Rizzoli
International Publications, Inc., 2001

Baten, Lea. "Japanese Kamo and
Kimekomi Dolls". *Doll Reader*. Nov., 1988

Brackman, Barbara. *Encyclopedia of Pieced
Quilt Patterns*. Compiled by Barbara
Brackman. Paducah: American Quilter's
Society, 1993

Connolly, Shane. *The Secret Language of
Flowers*. New York: Rizzoli International
Publications, Inc., 2004

Henderson, B. L. K. *Wonder Tales of Old
Japan*. London: P. Alla & Co., 1924

Lehner, Ernst and Johanna. *Folklore and
Symbolism of Flowers, Plants and Trees*.
New York: Dover Publications, Inc., 2003

Malone, Maggie. *5,500 Quilt Block Designs*.
New York: Sterling Publishing Co., 2003

Niehaus, Theodore F. *A Field Guide to
Pacific States Wildflowers*: Washington,
Oregon, California and Adjacent Areas.
Boston: Houghton Mifflin, 1998.

Nisizawa, Tekiho (Translated by S.
Sakabe). *Japanese Folk-Toys*. Tourist
Library: 26. Japanese Government
Railways, 1939

Perez, Louis G. *Daily Life in Early Modern
Japan*. Westport, Connecticut: Greenwood
Press, 2002

*Simon and Schuster's Complete Guide to
Plants and Flowers*. Ed. Frances Perry. New
York: Simon and Schuster, 1974

Suess, Barbara. *Japanese Temari*.
Elmhurst (Chicago): Breckling Press, 2007

Yamada, Tokubei. *Japanese Dolls*. Tokyo:
Japan Travel Bureau, 1964.

## Japanese Temari by Barbara B. Suess

How can anything that looks so intricate be so simple! Try it out and see!
With little more than a needle and thread, Barbara B. Suess shows you
how to make beautiful Japanese temari balls in dozens of colors and
patterns. Perfect for stitching on the go, the balls make beautiful gifts
and are wonderful home-dec accessories. Requiring few materials and
just a little practice, *Japanese Temari* offers 25 designs to choose from.
At every step, there are color drawings that show you exactly what to
do, as well as gorgeous photos to inspire you.

For more information visit www.brecklingpress.com or call 800-951-7936